I0796686

The Sun and the Moon

Emily Kington

Contents

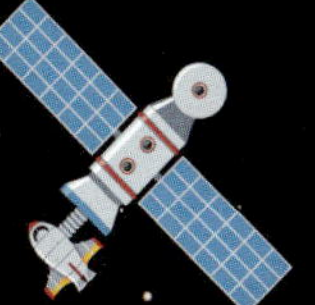

Words that appear in **bold** are explained in the glossary

Discover more at **www.hungrytomato.com**

Sun and Moon

The Sun provides light and heat to our whole **solar system.** Its light helps us see other moons and planets.

Our Moon is the brightest object in our night sky.

The Moon doesn't produce light. It looks bright because it **reflects** light from the Sun.

Without the Sun our planet would be a gigantic icy rock.

Scientists think the Moon was made when an object smashed into Earth. Pieces of our planet flew off into space, stuck together and made the Moon!

How Far to the Sun?

The Sun is at the heart of our solar system. Planets and other space objects within the solar system travel around the Sun in what is called an **orbit**.

Ganymede

Europe

Moon

Mercury

Earth

Our Earth and Moon are about 93 million miles (150 million kilometers) from the Sun.

Venus

If you were able to travel to the Sun in a Jumbo Jet, it would take you about 19 years to get there!

Sun

Jupiter
Callisto
Uranus
Pluto
Neptune
Io
All of the planets stay at a set distance from the Sun because of a pulling force called **gravity**.
Triton
Titan
Saturn
Mars
Our Sun is about four and a half billion years old and it should live for at least another 5 billion years... that's very old!

The Sun

The Sun is very important to life on Earth. It provides energy to grow the plants that we need for food and **oxygen**. It also helps to keep us warm!

The Sun is sooooo hot that there is nothing we can compare it to here on Earth. Its center can reach 27 million degrees Fahrenheit (15 million °C).

The Sun is a star. Stars create heat and light. You can see lots of stars in the sky, but they are all much further away.

The Sun may look like fire, but it isn't. It's mostly made up of two kinds of **gas**: *hydrogen* and *helium*.

We use sunscreen to protect us from harmful rays from the Sun, that could damage our skin.

The Earth's Orbit

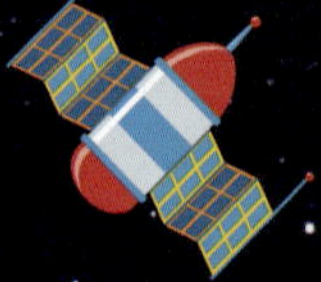

It takes Earth 365 days to orbit the Sun, that is one whole year! You can't feel it, but the Earth is zooming very quickly through space, even as you read this!

The Earth is speeding around the Sun at roughly 18.5 miles (30 kilometers) per second. That's incredibly fast!

In one orbit, the Earth will travel about 584 million miles (940 million kilometers). Phew!

The Earth orbits the Sun in an oval shape. This means that it is not always the same distance away from the Sun.

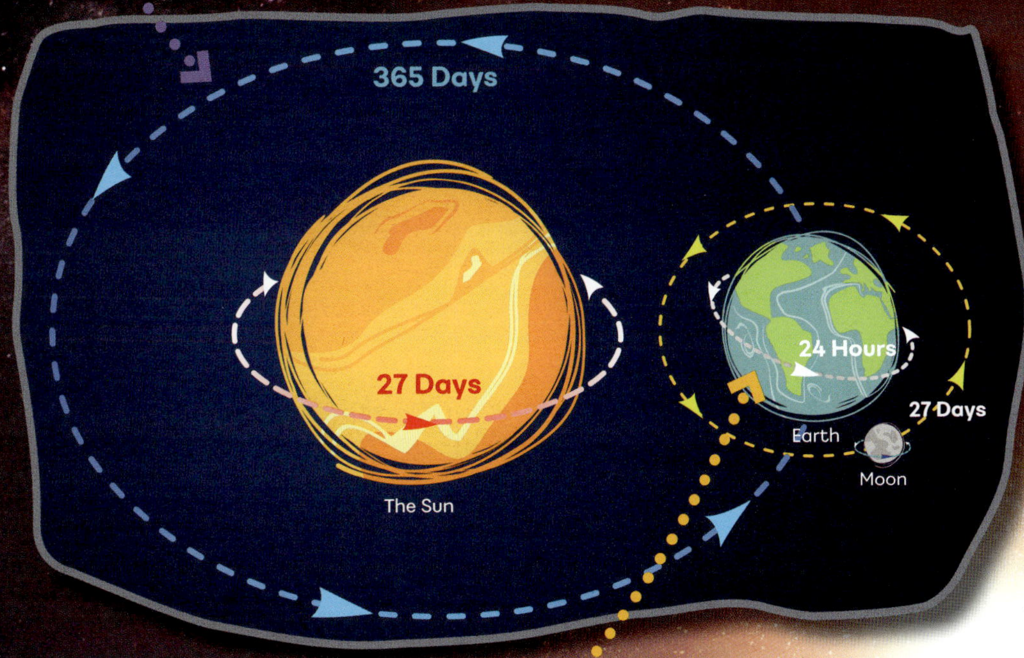

While it orbits the Sun, the Earth also spins around. It makes one full **rotation** every day.

The Moon

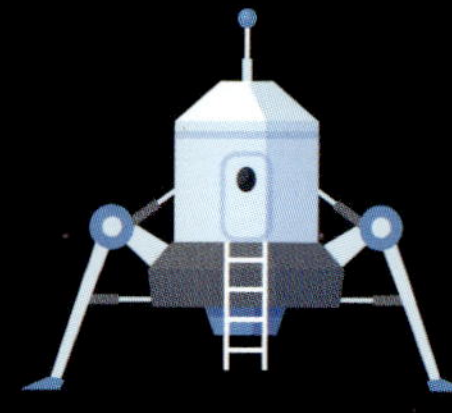

On 20th July 1969, *Neil Armstrong* and *Buzz Aldrin* became the first humans to set foot on the Moon, as part of the *Apollo 11* mission.

Once launched, it took 76 hours for Apollo 11 to travel 240,000 miles (386,243 kilometers), to enter the Moon's orbit.

We are still learning new things about the Moon. In 2020, NASA's mission SOFIA found proof that there is water on the Moon!
During their moon walk, Armstrong and Aldrin left a message that said, "We came in peace for all mankind"
The Moon's surface has mountains and lots of **craters,** and is covered in powdery soil, pebbles and rocks.

The Moon's Orbit

As Earth orbits the Sun, the Moon travels around Earth. It takes 27 days for the Moon to complete its orbit.

As it orbits, the Moon appears to be different shapes when viewed from Earth. We call these shapes the *Phases of the Moon*.

The Moon has phases because the Sun lights certain areas of the Moon at different stages of its orbit. From Earth, we only see the sunlit parts.

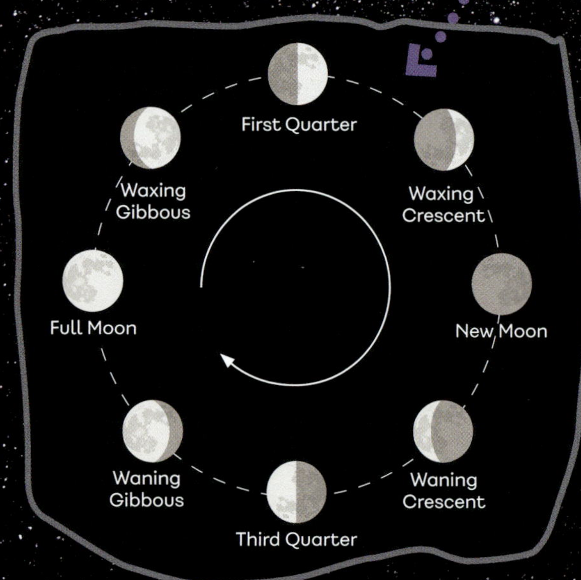

When full sunlight hits the Moon's surface, it can make it very hot, with temperatures reaching 260 °F (127 °C).
The Moon's orbit affects the **tides** of our seas and oceans.

Daytime

As Earth rotates, the Sun shines on the half of the planet that is facing it, providing it with daylight.

The Sun appears to come up in the morning and go down at night-time, as the Earth spins towards and away from the Sun.

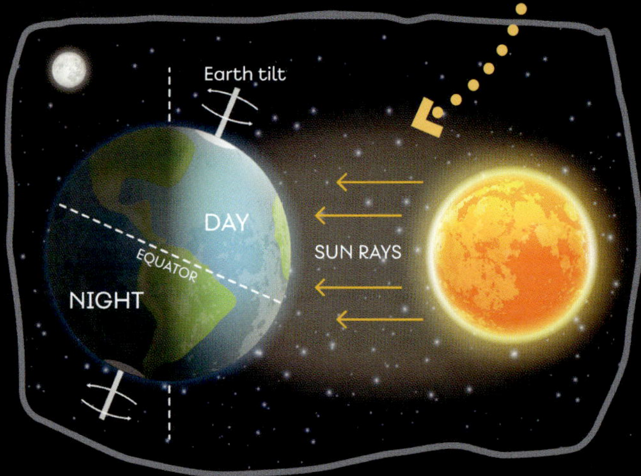

This side of the Earth is in shadow, and it is night-time.

During the day, the Sun's energy keeps our planet warm and gives us **natural light.**

Since it is night in some parts of the world while it is day in others, different places have different **time zones**.

Sometimes you can see the Moon during daytime too. This depends on its position and how much light from the Sun it is reflecting.

Night-time

As Earth rotates away from the Sun it starts to fall into darkness. The Moon provides some light by reflecting the Sun's rays.

Using electricity, we can make **artificial light** to help us see in the dark.

Have you noticed that it's cooler at night than it is in the daytime? This is because there are no Sun rays producing warmth.

Some night-time animals, like owls, have big eyes that pick up tiny rays of light to help them see in the dark

In most places around the world, nights are longest in the winter and shortest in the summer.

Seasons

Most places on Earth have four seasons throughout the year. We experience changes to the light, weather and nature in each season, all because of the Sun!

Earth rotates at a tilted angle as it orbits the Sun. So, at different times of the year some parts of Earth lean closer to the sun and other parts will be further away.

21 March
SPRING
WINTER
22 June
22 December
SUMMER
AUTUMN
23 September
When part of the Earth is leaning fully towards the Sun, it will be summer, and when it is leaning furthest away it will be winter.
Some places don't have four seasons. Areas around the **equator** stay warm all year!

Eclipses 

An eclipse occurs when an object in space, like a moon or a planet, blocks another object from view. On Earth we have Solar and Lunar eclipses.

A solar eclipse takes place when the Moon travels in front of the Sun, blocking some, or all of it, from view.

When the Sun is completely covered, we call it a *Total Eclipse*.

A lunar eclipse happens when the Sun, Moon and Earth are positioned in a straight line, with the Earth in the middle.
A lunar eclipse is sometimes called a *Blood Moon*, because it makes the Moon look red.
You should never look directly at a solar eclipse. It may look dark, but the Sun's rays could still damage your eyes!

Glossary

artificial light – man-made light, usually produced using electricity.

crater - a large hole in the ground, which has been caused by something hitting it, or by an explosion.

equator – an imaginary line around the middle of Earth's surface, at an equal distance from the North and South Poles.

gas - a substance that is neither solid or liquid and has no fixed shape. Many gases are invisible.

gravity - a pulling force that works across space. It's the same force that causes an object to fall when you drop it.

natural light – light produced by the Sun.

orbit - the path taken by one object circling around another object in space.

oxygen – is a gas in the air that we need to breathe.

reflects – when light bounces off the surface of an object, it is reflected.

rotation (rotate) – when something spins around a point located at its center.

solar system – the solar system contains all of the planets, dwarf planets, moons, and other objects that travel around the Sun.

tides – the regular change in the level of the sea on the shore.

time zones - areas of the world that are divided up according to what time they keep. Some time zones are behind or ahead of others by multiple hours.

Picture Credits
(abbreviations: t = top; b = bottom; m = middle; l = left; r = right; bg = background)

Shutterstock: Aphelleon 4bg; AZSTARMAN 23m; Baranov E 14bg; d3verro 1tr, 4tr, 6tm, 10tr, 14tr, 18t, 20tm, 22tm; Designua 21tr; diluck 11m; Dima Zel 12bg; Elena Zajchikova 20bg; Everett Collection 12ml; Feng Yu 18m; FlashMovie 16bg; Fred Mantel 23t; Gilda Villarreal 8bg; Kyle Cleary 24bg; Lijphoto 17r; Redsapphire 14bl; Rido 9br; Romolo Tavani 1bg; Romolo Tavani 22bg; Sahara Prince 4br; Siberian Art 16bl; Skorzewiak 2bg; Sunflowerr 6bg; Triff 8bm; Vadim Sadovski 10bg; VikiVector 3tm, 8tm, 12tm, 16tm, 24tr; VladKK 19tl; Yaska 20ml; Yindee (astronaut cartoons); zef art 18bg.

First published in Great Britain in 2021 by Hungry Tomato Ltd
F1, Old Bakery Studios, Blewetts Wharf, Malpas Road, Truro, Cornwall, TR1 1QH, UK

A CIP catalog record for this book is available from the British Library